banana

guava

orange

mango

pineapple

avocado pear

tangerine

passion fruit

For Emma, Linda, Nadine and Yewande

*The author would like to thank everyone who helped her research this book, especially Wanjiru and Nyambura from the Kenyan Tourist Office, and Achieng from the Kenyan High Commission.*

*The children featured in this book are from the Luo tribe of south-west Kenya.*

Copyright © 1994 Eileen Browne
Dual Language Copyright © 1999 Mantra Lingua
This edition published 2019

First published in 1994 by
Walker Books Ltd

Published by
Mantra Lingua
Global House
303 Ballards Lane
London N12 8NP
www.mantralingua.com

Printed in Letchworth, UK. PE240619PB07194777

# HANDA'NIN SÜRPRİZİ

## HANDA'S SURPRISE

Eileen Browne

*Turkish translation by* Kelâmi Dedezade

MANTRA
LINGUA

Handa arkadaşı Akeyo için sepete yedi tane nefis meyva koydu.

Handa put seven delicious fruits in a basket for her friend, Akeyo.

Arkadaşının hayret edeceğini düşünerek Akeyo'nun köyüne doğru yola çıktı.

She will be surprised, thought Handa as she set off for Akeyo's village.

Acaba en çok hangi meyvayı beğenecek?

I wonder which fruit she'll like best?

Sarı, yumuşak muzu mu beğenecek ...

Will she like the soft yellow banana ...

Yoksa tatlı kokulu guavayı mı?

or the sweet-smelling guava?

Yuvarlak, sulu portakalı mı beğenecek ...

Will she like the round juicy orange ...

Yoksa pişmiş, kırmızı mangoyu mu?

or the ripe red mango?

Sivri yapraklı ananası mı beğenecek ...

Will she like the spiky-leaved pineapple ...

Yeşil, kaymak gibi avakadoyu mu ...

the creamy green avocado ...

Yoksa mor, keskin passion meyvasını mı?

or the tangy purple passion-fruit?

Which fruit will Akeyo like best?

Akeyo en çok hangi meyvayı beğenecek?

"Hello, Akeyo," said Handa. "I've brought you a surprise."

"Merhaba Akeyo," dedi Handa. "Sana bir sürpriz getirdim."

"Mandalina!" dedi Akeyo. "En beğendiğim meyva."
"MANDALİNA MI?" dedi Handa. "İşte sürpriz budur!"

"Tangerines!" said Akeyo. "My favourite fruit."
"TANGERINES?" said Handa. "That *is* a surprise!"